Tom,

This made me
think of you.

Love,

T x

CARBECUE

THE COMPLETE GUIDE TO COOKING ON A CAR ENGINE

By Alfred Cary

First published in the United Kingdom by Alfred Cary Publishing, 2014
This paperback edition published in 2014

ISBN 978-0-9930756-0-5

All photography by Alfred Cary except: Joanna Cary (9, 46 top right, 47, 62 top left and bottom right, 68, all of 69) Adrian Houston (bottom of page 17) Henry Frost (26-27) Mary Alexander (40-41), Kieran Hamilton (50-51), Lutz Braum (84-85)
The following images are reproduced with kind permission of Forest Wanderer (64-65)

Contents

Introduction

Last year I was sitting in a service station, facing a tricky decision. Sausage, egg and beans? Burger and chips? Or an overpriced sandwich? None of these processed foods appealed to me in the slightest. It got me thinking; there must be a better way, a way to eat delicious hot food, on the move, at your own convenience. This triggered the idea that cooking in its simplest form was just applying heat to food. Where could you get heat from? A car engine. It seemed so simple. Contain food securely in tinfoil packages, and then place them on the engine, and the heat would cook the food as you drive.

And so Carbecue was born. On a return journey from Edinburgh, my siblings and I stopped at the local butcher, full of enthusiasm, and excitement about what lay ahead. We bought a handful of lamb chops, a few potatoes and a couple of green beans. Wrapping them up very thoroughly in tinfoil, and carefully putting them on the engine, we set off. I don't think I have ever been so excited about a meal as I was that day. The thought of actually cooking food using my car was extraordinary. About 100 miles down the road we stopped for lunch, and unwrapped the piping hot package with a nervous excitement. Inside were beautifully cooked lamb chops, with steam billowing out. It made for such a jolly lunch. We ate and laughed and dreamt up new recipes for what we would cook next.

A few Google searches later and I found that cooking on car engines was a known phenomenon in USA, and that it had started during hard times, as a way for truckers to cook without paying for electricity to heat their ovens. However, I found nothing inspiring in my searches, so I began cooking using my engine more and more. From sirloin, to fish, and from pigeon to shrimp, I wasn't afraid to try anything, and the results were very pleasing and I was having such fun doing it. I have always found car journeys great for thinking and it was during one of these journeys that I decided that I needed to spread the word about engine cooking. Whether inspired, or foolish optimism, I would have fun along the way, and would no doubt learn a lot.

So I began to juggle my university degree at Edinburgh with a recipe once a week. In typical student manner funds were very low, but I spared no expense on quality ingredients and a good camera. I soon found that cooking times varied between cars, so I attached a cooking thermometer to my dashboard and wired it up through the window, under the bonnet and into the food. This allowed me to see exactly when the food was perfectly cooked from the comfort of my own car and saved time checking the food. Unfortunately, I do not recommend you use a thermometer as you may pierce the tinfoil package in doing so. I made the decision very early that I would keep everything 'in-house', largely dictated by the fact that I couldn't afford anyone else's help. I used friends where I could, and my sister is a fantastic freelance chef, which has been a brilliant help. I would have loved to have someone who knew about photography helping me, but I realised I would just have to learn. After about four or five months of sporadic engine cooking, and a slipping educational record, I had compiled about 20 recipes, having tried them on my car, refined them, and photographed them. Now all I had to do was make them into a book. I hadn't really considered how to do this. And within an hour of starting I quickly realised that often my photos were inadequate, my writing debatable and wit non-existent (despite clear attempts). So I postponed progress to the summer, where I had a strict timeline of 4 months to complete the book. And here I am with one month left, with good photographs, better writing, and wit still non-existent (with now, clear desperate attempts).

I have tried to make the book as visually strong as I could, in order to prove to people just how successful cooking on a car is. Every photo taken of food in this book has been cooked on a car and no shortcuts have been taken. That was always very important to me to reflect a fair image of a Carbecue.

I guess that it is only natural that I fell into writing this book. My father is an entrepreneurial engineer, who has helped start over one hundred companies. My mother is an inspired cook, who has always provided home cooked food and told us of the importance of knowing where our food comes from. My sister went to Ballymaloe, and has become a brilliant freelance chef. My brother works as an engineer for a food company, producing environmentally-friendly food packaging. And my other sister loves eating. So I guess that along the way I picked up an appetite for both engineering and cooking but committed to neither, thus leaving me somewhere in the middle. And Carbecue seems to be the creation of this mix.

Maybe I've driven in my car alone for too long with my thoughts overtaking me, but it seems to me service stations are largely depressing places with inadequate food options. With the exception of Westmoreland Tebay Services on the M6, which is a wonderful farm shop with locally produced food and a butcher on site, service stations produce substandard, greasy, pre-packaged food that doesn't appeal. Unfortunately, they hold a monopoly and twenty years ago this was what the demand for food was in this country. In recent times there has been somewhat of a food revolution, and inspiring work from celebrity chefs like Jamie Oliver and Hugh Fearnley-Whittingstall has changed the way we think about food. Now there is a real focus on cooking sustainably produced food, from scratch, and this book tries to encompass these beliefs wherever possible.

I can practically hear you say, "Where's the sustainability in cooking on a car engine? Surely, if anything that's adding to the problem?" Well, no: what I advocate is that you should never drive to cook, but only cook when driving. So if you are doing a journey anyway then it is entirely possible and highly likely that en route or on arrival you may want to eat. In this case it is very sensible and more sustainable to cook using your car engine. If your engine is going to be producing enough heat to cook on anyway, then you may as well use it, rather than use additional energy when you get home to power your oven.

In my car I have now commandeered an old wooden box, which I keep useful things like salt, pepper, paprika, a sharp knife, a few glasses, plates, knives and forks. I have found that it is brilliant, particularly when setting out on a journey away from home to have some staples in the car so that I can cook food from scratch whenever the opportunity arises. You never know when a carbecue expedition may spring up on you.

It is worth pointing out that you can cook on any petrol or diesel car engine. And although I have never cooked using a hybrid car, I have come across people who have, but they have warned me that cooking times must be extended. Many modern cars are covered in plastic, but ultimately the engine is made of metal and so the heated bits do still exist but are just harder to find. Unfortunately, cooking on fully electric cars isn't possible, as they don't produce nearly enough heat.

I believe in sustainably produced food, cooked from scratch, and all the recipes in the book demonstrate this. These are just some of the many recipes that could be cooked using a car engine, and are by no means definitive. Hopefully, this book will inspire others to try their own recipes and do send them in to **www.carbecue.co.uk** so that we can all share your experiences.

Instructions:

If you've got to this section of the book I hope that you are now enthusiastically awaiting your first Carbecue. All that remains is, how? How do I go about this? This next section will explain everything that you need to know, from the basic steps to the helpful tips that I have learnt along the way.

I want to keep this as simple as I can and honestly there isn't much to it. So if you follow these instructions then you can't really go wrong. The general principle is that you want to wrap food well to completely seal it with good quality tinfoil, before adding it to the hottest part of your car engine. I'm going to do all the examples with reference to the roast beef recipe. It is a very simple recipe and therefore is a good guide for following without the complications of culinary extravagance.

The first thing you need to do is wrap your beef in thick, good quality tinfoil. To the right are photos of the process, but ultimately you need to place the beef in the centre of the tinfoil and wrap a single layer around the beef, so that it overlaps at the top. Then turn this tinfoil package over, and place it in the middle of a second sheet of tinfoil. Wrap this around, making sure it overlaps at the top again. You now have a double sealed package, which is impenetrable from any oil sitting on your engine. This package is now ready

to place on your engine for cooking. But how do you know where to cook it on your engine?

Every engine is different, but all engines produce a large amount of waste heat. The idea for Carbecue is to harness this waste heat to cook with, and we therefore want to find the hottest part of an engine to cook on. I am not petrolhead, and really don't know lots about cars. I know roughly how they work but certainly wouldn't be able to identify parts on a car, although since I started this book my knowledge has become more extensive. But what I would say is that this is certainly not necessary.

To find the perfect place to cook on your car engine, I would recommend driving for five minutes, stopping and then opening up your car bonnet. Have a look and just hold your hand a couple of centimetres above parts of the engine. You should be able to clearly find the areas that are the hottest, which will always be metal. You cannot cook on any plastic parts, as they will never get hot enough. These areas will usually be above the spark plugs, or on the exhaust manifold. It is these areas, which are most suitable for cooking on. You can then place your tinfoil package containing your food on these identified spots.

NB It is very important that you identify the accelerator linkage on a car and make sure that the food doesn't interfere with this at all. You can do this with the engine switched off. Have someone push the accelerator down while looking at the engine. You should see a small wire move. This is the accelerator linkage. Make sure that at no point any packages placed on the car interfere with this, and are sufficiently secured so that they will not move and obstruct this wire.

When you place your packages on the engine it will be necessary to secure these in some way to it, so that they don't move. To do this I use short lengths of metal wire just a few inches long. To get these you could cut lengths off a coat hanger or just visit any DIY store. It is important that you do not forcefully stuff the package in around parts of the car, as you may damage both the package and the car. Bend these wires around your tinfoil packages and secure them lightly around parts of the engine, ensuring that they do not pull on them but are just there in case the positioning of the tinfoil package fails.

You now drive as far as the recipe suggests or until your meat reaches the desired internal temperature, so in the case of the roast beef between two and half to three and half hours. On arrival, switch off the engine, open the bonnet, and allow it to cool for a few minutes. Approach the engine with caution, as it will remain hot for many hours, so I would recommend using an oven glove or tea towel. With clean hands take the package out of the car and unwrap it. This is always the most exciting bit for me and you should now have a beautifully cooked joint, but be sure to test it. If you spot that your package has been split or has a hole in it somewhere then it is important that you do not eat anything from that package, as it may be contaminated.

If for some reason the food needs a little longer, then rewrap the meat using clean hands with fresh tinfoil and re-attach it to the engine using the steps outlined earlier. However, your food should be cooked so at this point you can now enjoy the meal. I cannot tell you how satisfying this moment is.

You now have all the means and knowledge to complete a Carbecue recipe, but here are the key points just to help you out.

Key Points:

- Use the best quality tinfoil you can find.
- Double wrap the food in tinfoil
- Drive for 5 minutes and then hold your hand above the engine to find the hottest parts.
- Place the tinfoil packages on the hottest parts of the engine and secure them using short lengths of wire.
- Drive for the suggested time in the recipe, and then check whether the food is cooked.
- If it is not, rewrap the food in new tinfoil and continue your journey.
- All cars are different so timings may vary, so getting to know your car is very useful.

A Brief History.

The exact origins of cooking on cars are unknown but it can be said that it wasn't soon after the invention of the car that people were cooking on them. It seems that where there is heat there is cooking and the car was no different.

The earliest recordings of cooking on engines were the use of the steam trains in the UK. One of the jobs of the apprentice on board was to heat two pots of tea. When pulling into a station he would take one pot off and place it on the rear of the platform as the train went through. The staff at the back of the train would then pick up the teapot on the move. Although not exactly gourmet cooking, it is the first example of harnessing the wasted heat produced by an engine for a usable means. Engine cooking's next great step was the invention and popularisation of the car. During these times, both in Britain and in the US, cooking on car engines took place.

In Britain, Rolls-Royce motorcars in the early 20th Century were sold as a chassis only, meaning it was an engine and a drive train mounted on a rolling frame. From there it went to a coachbuilder, who would allow an endless list of options and customisation to the motorcars, specifically designed for the customers needs. One such option was to have a cooking plate fitted onto the engine to make the process of cooking on your engine even easier. It highlights the popularity and ease of cooking on engines at the time, but somewhere over the next 80 years the art largely died out, slowly being replaced by inadequate service stations.

In 1908, the Ford Model T went on sale and was specifically designed to be affordable to everyday Americans, such as the factory workers at Ford. This car was incredibly successful and by 1929, 1 in every 6 Americans owned a car. The great depression then shook the world and during this time the second hand car market wasn't exactly booming, so people would often be stuck with cars as their only valuable possession. As people drove from town to town in search of work, they would cook on their car engine as they went. It meant that on arrival to a town, or even to their own homes, there was no need to pay for the electricity or fuel to cook food, but they could harness this otherwise wasted heat source produced on every car engine. It was convenient, logical and entirely sensible. It saved money and produced delicious hot food.

At a similar time, the British Army were also using their tanks to cook on. If they were in the desert they would just cook fried eggs straight off the metal plating using the heat from the sun. However, they would also pierce cans of

MaConochie's Meat & Veg, and put them into the engine compartment.[1] They would then nicely heat up and would be ready to eat not long after. And in typical British fashion they would also use this method for heating pots of tea.

Engine cooking in modern life has taken many interesting turns. It has featured on Top Gear, where they cooked a rack of lamb with market vegetables, dressed in olive oil and Mediterranean herbs. Hugh Fearnley-Whittingstall very successfully cooked a carp on the engine of his Land Rover, describing cooking on a car engine as "an irresistible idea". Keith Floyd cooked "Steak a la Toyota" on his car engine saying, "Fantastic for those daft enough to try". The MythBusters tried a Thanksgiving meal with great results. The Daily Mail featured an article about cooking a roast while driving round the M25. These moments of fame for engine cooking have often been short-lived but each and every example has proved that it works fantastically well and that people are very willing to try it.

In my travels I have spoken to people who have used the mainframes of commercial computers to heat their sandwiches on for lunch, just to slightly melt the cheese. Lisa Casali wrote an inspiring book about the benefits of cooking in a dishwasher, which also harnesses a wasted heat source. Maori women would lower flax bags, containing food, into the hot springs and leave them there to cook. What I have found is that wherever there is heat, people can and will cook on it. Car engines are no different and I hope that this book does justice to the brilliant phenomenon of engine cooking.

1. Unfortunately you can no longer pierce a can and put it on the engine block, because these days cans are mostly lined with a thin layer of plastic.

AW.677

- Short Journeys -

NO PARKING

15 Minute Drive
Serves: 2

The shepherd's steak sandwich refers to the origins of the Roquefort cheese, which is used in this dish. The story goes that a shepherd was eating his bread and cheese for lunch in a cave, when a beautiful girl distracted him. He chased after the girl, but left his cheese behind. He returned one month later to find that his cheese was covered in mould, penicillium roqueforti, and had turned in to what we now know as Roquefort.

As steak is a prime cut of meat it is important that we cook it as quickly as we can. It is therefore crucial that you drive for five minutes before putting the steaks on to cook, so the engine is piping hot. This combo of the subtle flavor from the marinated beef, to the rich Roquefort cheese mixes unusually with a horseradish garnishing. My sister said "way too much going on here", when I announced my plans, but one bite soon had her eating her words (and the steak sandwich).

The Shepherd's Steak Sandwich

Place the steaks into a shallow dish suitable for marinating. To this add equal amounts of olive oil, soy sauce, Worcestershire sauce, and sherry/balsamic vinegar. Then add the mustard and mix well. Leave this to marinate for at least 1 hour but ideally leave overnight. When you're ready to set off on your journey, take the steak out of the marinade and place each steak on its own bit of tinfoil, taking a little of the marinade with you. Add to this some crushed garlic and finely diced onions. Wrap the tinfoil firmly around the steaks and drive for at least 5 minutes before adding the steaks. They should only take 10 minutes for a minute/feather steak or 15 minutes for a thicker rump steak. When you reach you destination, unwrap your steaks quickly to ensure that they don't continue to cook, slice finely and add them to the ciabatta loaf. Add to this the mixed salad, chunks of Roquefort cheese, and horseradish.

Ingredients

2 well-aged rump, minute or feather steaks (try to get hold of thin cut steaks for quicker cooking)
1 tbsp of olive oil
1 tbsp of soy sauce
1 tbsp of Worcestershire sauce
1 tbsp of sherry/ balsamic vinegar
2 tsp of mustard
1 garlic clove
1 small onion
2 ciabatta loaves
30g of mixed salad
Roquefort cheese
horseradish (p82)

Garlic Prawns with Avocado and Summer Leaves

20 Minute Drive
Serves: 2

Ingredients

20 peeled and deveined prawns
1 garlic clove, finely chopped
a knob of butter
a handful of fresh parsley, chopped
a squeeze of lemon juice, to serve
handful of watercress
handful of summer leaves
1 avocado sliced
half a red onion, finely sliced

Ok so I'll admit this recipe is not exactly typical to the Carbecue model. In fact many people have said, surely you could just buy the prawns pre-cooked and have a picnic rather than a Carbecue. And it is a fair point. I'd argue that a salad is much nicer with a hot ingredient, but I'd also say that this is really an entry level to Carbecue. So if you want to test out your car for the first time, or just this book in general, then I would recommend this one. It's very easy to do, and there is only one primary ingredient to cook on a short journey, and therefore less that can go wrong.

Take the prawns and mix them with the chopped garlic and parsley. Place them on tinfoil and then add a knob of butter and squeeze a little lemon juice on them. Fold them up in two layers of tinfoil, place them on the engine and drive for 20 minutes. Put all the summer leaves and watercress in a bowl and add the avocado, sliced red onion, pine nuts and the garlic prawns to the leaves. Admire. Pat yourself on the back.

Eat.

Salmon Fillets

Served with Samphire and Dill Relish.

25 Minute Drive
Serves: 4

Fish lends itself very well to being cooked on a car engine, because the tinfoil keeps all the moisture in, and you end up with a steaming effect. Indeed, an episode of "A Cook on the Wild Side", Hugh Fearnley-Whittingstall's first TV series prior to the more famous River Cottage, featured Hugh cooking fish using the engine of his Land Rover Defender with wonderful results. So with the confidence of success elsewhere, I set off on a 25-minute journey and cooked these salmon fillets with a handful of samphire and glug of cucumber and dill sauce. A little slice of lemon to garnish the salmon is recommended to complete this culinary delight.

Ingredients

4 salmon fillets
a squeeze of lemon
a twist or two of pepper
1 twist of black pepper, freshly ground
a handful of samphire
a knob of butter
cucumber and dill sauce , to serve (p82)

Season the salmon with a squeeze of lemon and a twist or two of pepper. Wrap the fillets individually in tinfoil, ensuring they are double wrapped, with an additional layer on top. Also fold the Samphire in a double layer of tinfoil with accompanying butter. Place on the engine and drive for 25 minutes. On arrival remove the salmon and samphire from their tinfoil packages, and serve with the pre-prepared cucumber and dill sauce (pg. 82).

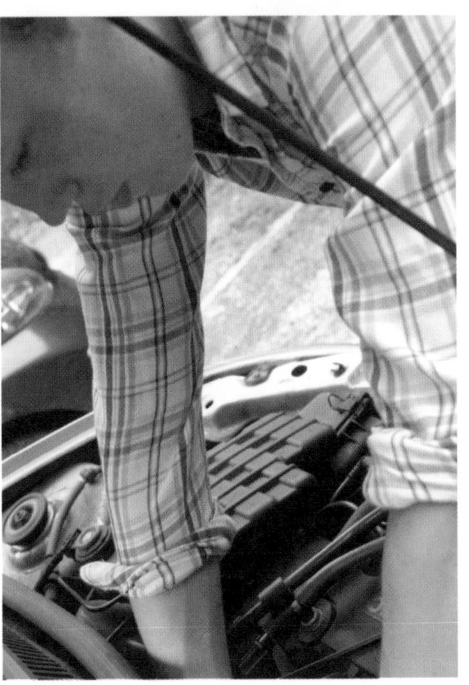

Ford
DURATEC

DRR 417B

intelligently is an art."
-François La Rochefoucauld

25-40 Minute Drive
Serves: 4, as a starter

This is a really good recipe to try for your first ever Carbecue. This baked Camembert is very simple and easy to cook, and good as a little snack to keep a carload of you going. I personally love the garlic and rosemary flavours, but I have an unusually high resistance to garlic. I'd therefore be wary about using this little number on a first date but maybe save it for a family holiday. I recommend eating this with a fresh loaf of bread or alternatively a ciabatta or even a baked potato.

Baked Camembert

Ingredients

250g of Camembert cheese in wooden box
2 cloves of garlic, sliced
5 sprigs of rosemary
A baguette, to serve

Remove any plastic packaging from the Camembert, but leave it in the bottom half of its wooden box. Make about 15 small slits in the top of the cheese with a knife. Stuff the garlic slices and rosemary sprigs into these slits. Take this rather beautiful-looking cheese and double wrap it in tinfoil leaving it inside its wooden base. Place on the engine and drive for a minimum of 25 minutes but anything up to 40 minutes is fine depending on how runny you like it. Serve with baguette.

30 Minute Drive
Serves: 2

I think that pigeon is such underrated meat. You should be able to get hold of it from any decent butcher, or a quick trip round woodland with an air rifle is another method. Providing it is cooked no more than medium rare it oozes succulence, and is very visually appealing. I wouldn't recommend anything more than a 30-minute journey otherwise it will become bland and dry. The mushrooms won't cook through but will just warm and they should provide a more earthy taste, and complemented with the walnuts, watercress, and cottage cheese this lunchtime treat can't be refused. I recommend serving it on a farmhouse loaf.

Ingredients

4 pigeon breasts
3 button mushrooms, chopped
2 sprigs of rosemary, finely chopped
watercress, to serve
crushed walnuts, to serve
cottage cheese, to serve
a farmhouse loaf, sliced

WoodPigeon Sandwich served with Walnuts, Mushrooms and Watercress.

Finely chop the rosemary sprigs and sprinkle over the pigeon breasts. Wrap them in a double layer of tinfoil ensuring that pigeon breasts are not on top of one another. Chop the mushrooms and also fold into a separate tinfoil package. Place these on the engine and drive for 30 minutes. On arrival slice the bread and add the cottage cheese, the watercress and the pigeon breasts to the bread. Sprinkle the crushed walnuts over the top and then you're ready to eat.

- Mid-distance Journeys -

40 Minute Drive
Serves: 2

It is important not to overcomplicate the cooking process, and cooking is as much about enjoying the food produced as the method to get there, which may seem odd when using car engines. This recipe really displays this philosophy by being straightforward to complete, effortlessly elegant, and really tasty. Melted mozzarella is one of my great weaknesses. It's so goddamn good. I think my perfect day would be popping bubble wrap, eating melted mozzarella, while listening to David Attenborough talk, all with the smell of freshly cut grass lingering in the air. It only takes 40 minutes to get the mozzarella to the optimum molten level, worthy of making my perfect day a reality.

Ingredients

4 portobello mushrooms
15 to 20 leaves of fresh spinach, torn
1 ball of mozzarella, grated
1 clove of garlic, minced
1 tbsp of breadcrumbs
a drizzle of olive oil
salt and pepper
sweet chilli jam (p86), to serve

Stuffed Portobello Mushrooms

Served with Mozzarella, Garlic and Spinach

Clean the mushrooms and take off the stems by hand. Combine the spinach, garlic, and mozzarella and then place them in the open top of the portobello mushrooms. Add the breadcrumbs, and season with salt and pepper, before putting a small drizzle of olive oil on top. Double wrap each mushroom in tinfoil, individually and place on the engine. Drive for 40 minutes before checking your mushrooms. The cheese should be nicely melted and ready to eat.

MADE IN
SHEFFIELD ENGLAND
STAINLESS
STEEL

45 Minute Drive
Serves: 2

This twist on a classic has a few interesting ingredients, that usually play a ten-minute game of hide and seek with me in the supermarket, but give them a lot of exciting flavours. On a bed of spinach, this dish oozes simplicity, but I have a crafty feeling people might be impressed you've cooked it on a car. Just a short 45-minute drive is perfect for this.

I always find there is something quite magical about eating fish by the seaside particularly if you've caught the fish yourself. I tried for nearly two hours to get a bite with no success. Then around the corner came a local fisherman who told me that I wouldn't have a hope of catching anything in this area. "Too rocky' ere", he said. I then pulled up my rod, rather embarrassed, only to find that my hook had been lost, no doubt to an incompetently tied knot. Fishing never was my strong suit, but on the plus side the local fishmonger got a bit of extra business.

Ingredients

1 whole seabass
3 lemongrass stalks, chopped
1 chilli, halved
1 large garlic clove, finely sliced
fresh ginger peeled and carved into thin strips
a drizzle of runny honey
a swirl of olive oil
a lemon
a large handful of spinach
a knob of butter
1 garlic glove, minced
sweet chilli jam (p86), to serve

Oriental Seabass on a Bed of Spinach

Gut and descale the sea bass and then wash, both inside and outside, and dry with a cloth. Deeply score the fish 5-6 times on each side and place on the tin foil. Firmly mix the lemongrass, chillies, garlic, ginger and honey, bruising the ingredients to release the flavours. Place the mixture inside the scores and inside the centre of the fish. Finish by squeezing lemon all over the fish, adding pepper and a swig of olive oil. Double wrap the foil around the fish. Meanwhile crush a clove of garlic, and mix with a large handful of spinach. Place on top of some fresh tinfoil and add a knob of butter and fold the parcel. Add both packages to the engine prioritising the sea bass into the hottest area of the engine and drive for 45 minutes.

45 Minute Drive
Serves: 1

For many of the meals, we don't exactly reinvent the wheel; we just make things that can be made in an oven and then do it in a car. But this one is fairly revolutionary. So hold onto your hats, as you prepare for this news (drum role inserted here) : we cook couscous in a pepper… Ok so it doesn't sound quite as glamorous as I might have built it up to be, but it is still pretty cool. Faced with the seemingly impossible task of containing water to cook couscous with on a car engine, I came up with the idea to cook it inside a pepper. Taking the top off a pepper creates a bowl, which can contain water and couscous. Add to this the heat of the engine and you've effectively got yourself a boiling pot. The results are magnificent, with cooked couscous and a softened pepper, to add to the concoction of ingredients that make this vegetarian dish a delicacy.

Ingredients

1 large red pepper
100g couscous
150ml of cold water
1 tbsp chopped fresh mint
4 spring onions, chopped
2 tbsp chopped fresh coriander
1 mango, peeled, finely chopped
2 tbsp olive oil
½ lemon, juice only
salt and pepper
pesto (p80), to serve

Couscous with Mango, Spring Onion and Red Pepper.

Take the red pepper and carefully cut the top off. Hollow out the middle and then put the uncooked couscous inside. Only fill the pepper to just over half way with the couscous. Add the cold water leaving just a centimetre at the top and then replace the 'lid' of the pepper. We use cold water so that the pepper can soften while the couscous cooks. Double wrap the pepper in tinfoil and be sure to hold it upright, so that the water doesn't spill. Put the package on the engine, and drive for 45 minutes. It may be sensible to do all your chopping at home and keep it in a bowl, but there's something quite satisfying about whipping out a chopping board and knife at a remote Carbecue area. Mix the chopped mint, coriander, spring onions, chopped mango, olive oil, lemon juice, and add to the, now delightfully cooked couscous. Chop the pepper and mix into the couscous

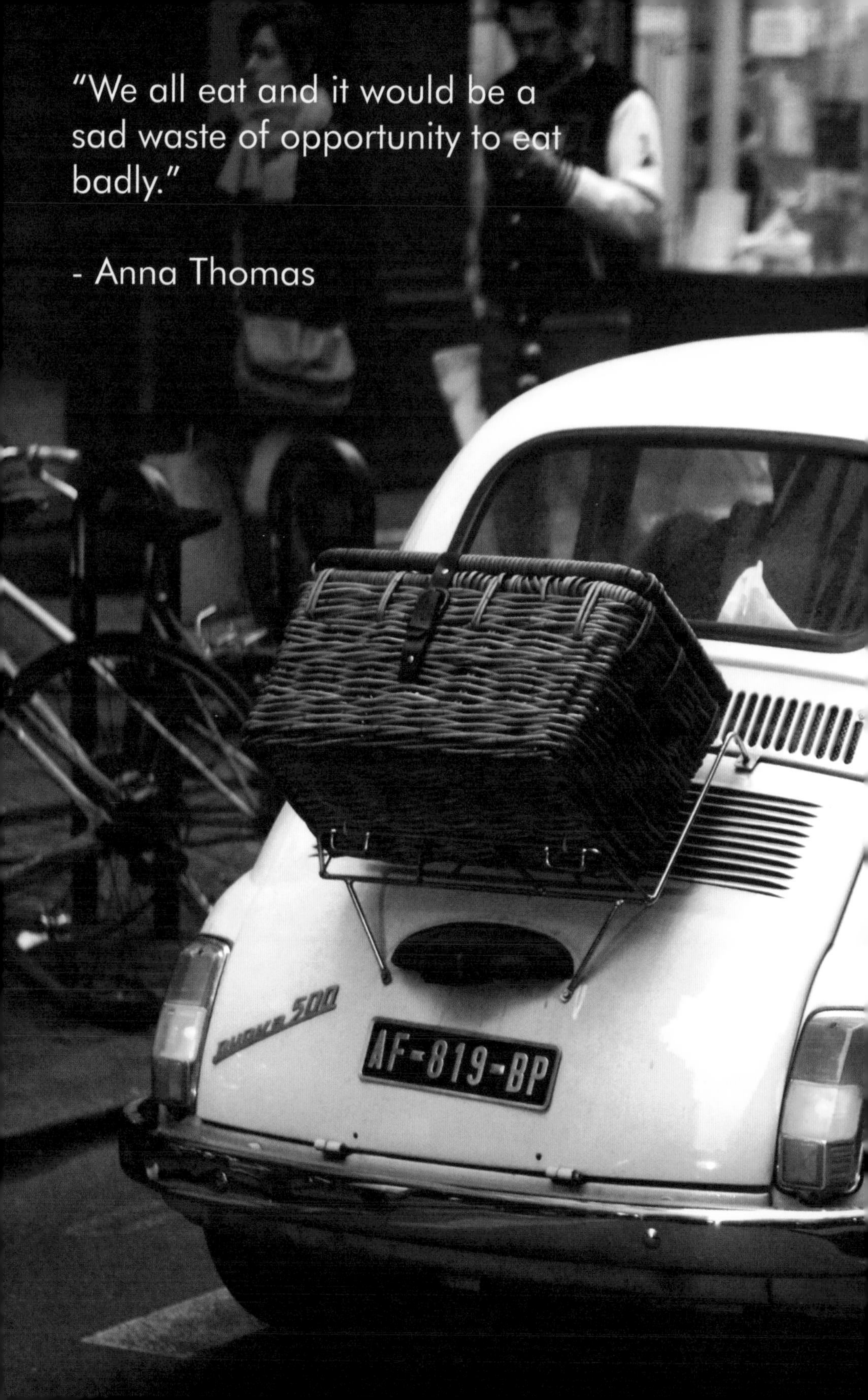

"We all eat and it would be a sad waste of opportunity to eat badly."

- Anna Thomas

35 Minute-1 Hour Drive
Serves: 2

The beauty of this supremely simple meal is that you can change the thickness of the burger to suit the length of your journey. A thin burger will be perfect for a 35-minute journey, but for a more substantial trip a hefty wedge of mince will be needed. A homemade beef burger is difficult to beat, so getting the right flavors is very important. This recipe has a strong undertone of coriander, with a sharp but not overpowering sensation of chilli and mustard that echoes through. I'm a massive spice wimp (can't eat a korma without sweating substantially) but still like this one! A side portion of peas is a very nice accompaniment and I just add a sizeable dollop of butter to them and heat them for the same amount of time as the burger.

Ingredients

250g beef steak mince
a handful of coriander, chopped
1 tbsp mustard
half an onion, finely chopped
fresh chilli, chopped
pepper
buns, to serve
choice of toppings
tomato salsa (p88)
gherkins
salad
finely sliced Gruyère or Edam (I like them better than Cheddar on a burger)

Put the mince, onion, mustard, coriander and chilli in a mixing bowl and add pepper too. Do not add salt at this point, as you will break down the fats and the meat will become very dry. Begin pressing all the ingredients through your fingers ensuring it is well mixed. Shape the burgers with regard to the length of your journey. For longer journeys make a fatter burger and for shorter journeys a thinner burger will be more suitable. The burger in the photo was for a 50-minute cooking time. Wrap in tinfoil individually or side-by-side but do not stack above one another or they will not cook evenly.

Pour the frozen peas into the tin foil folding the edges up to avoid spilling any. Add a generous knob of butter and then take the four corners of the tin foil and bring them all together and then twist them round. You should end up with a teardrop-looking package, which is then ready to put in the engine alongside the burgers. Drive for up to an hour depending on the thickness of your burger. Serve in a bun, with four choice of toppings.

THE DRIVE-THRU Beef Burger.

ENLEY
Dark

40 Minute Drive
Serves: 4

These tuna burgers are really quite a delightful change from the usual beef burgers. Similar to the beef burgers these have a versatile cooking time depending on how thick you make them. I always like a thick burger as it holds a little more moisture and gives you something to really wrap your teeth around. Although unnervingly green in colour, this only highlights the sharp flavors from the basil, mint and coriander. A refreshing throat tickle can be provided with a little red chilli for the spice lovers out there, although I certainly won't be adding any to my own (if I put too much pepper on a meal my eyes water).

You never know where you're going to end up for your lunch as the cooking times do vary slightly. Unfortunately I got caught up in a bit of city traffic but managed to find a great spot with the skate park on one side and a nature reserve on the other, which provided lunchtime entertainment as well as beautiful wildlife. In my travels throughout England, I have found that you are never more than 15 minutes from something very beautiful, from, say, a London Park, or an idyllic lake in Northumberland, which makes Carbecue the perfect excuse to visit some of these triumphs.

Ingredients

600g fresh tuna steak, sustainably sourced
a clutch of fresh basil, fresh mint and coriander
lemon zest, ½ a lemon
2 shallots
a red chilli(optional, in my case inconceivable) , to taste
salt and pepper
burger buns or ciabatta, to serve
tomato salsa (p88), to serve
a handful of rocket, to serve

Tuna Burgers with Basil, Mint and Coriander.

Finely chop the tuna, basil, mint, coriander, shallots, and add the lemon zest to a bowl. Mix well with your hands and then begin shaping your burgers into four equal sizes. I like my burgers nice and thick, but do this depending on how long your journey is. For a longer journey thicker burgers will obviously take longer. Season well before individually wrapping the burgers in tinfoil and placing in the fridge for half an hour (not strictly necessary) and then add them to the engine and drive for up to 1 hour depending on the thickness of the burgers you have made. When done remove from the engine, and add the burgers to the buns or ciabatta with the tomatoes and rocket.

1 Hour Drive
Serves: 2

This is an Ottolenghi-inspired infusion of flavours suitable for vegetarians. Carving out the insides of a romano pepper, the creamy cheeses are combined with a herb and nut filled mix, which is stuffed inside before placing on the engine for one hour to cook as you drive. Green chillies can be added to spice it up, and a dash of lime zest brings some additional flavour. A really refreshing meal perfect for a sunny afternoon or a spring day, served with some good quality bread or ciabatta.

Make a slice down the romano pepper and carefully remove the insides of the pepper without fully cutting it. Mix up all the remaining ingredients in a mixing bowl, before placing inside the romano pepper. Double wrap in tin foil, then add to the engine and drive for an hour. Remove from the engine and then look very pleased with yourself.

Ingredients

2 romano peppers
75g of ricotta
35g of mascarpone
a sprinkling of chopped pine nuts.
a healthy handful of parsley, chives and oregano finely chopped
the zest of a lemon, and a squeeze of juice
1 green chilli to taste
salt and pepper
ciabatta, to serve

Romano Peppers

Stuffed with Mascapone and Ricotta.

1 Hour Drive
Serves: 2

I cannot think of anything more manly in the world than eating a Nearly Full-English breakfast having cooked it using your car. I would recommend washing it down with some engine oil, chewing a few raw onions, while curling your handlebar moustache. Whether driving to work? Or recovering from a hangover? Or even indulging in a mid-afternoon snack? This is the ultimate no frills, no funny business cooking. Each of the components of this meal are individually wrapped, so space on the engine may be at a premium. It's important to prioritise the sausages, bacon and black pudding to be on the hottest parts of the engine, while the tomatoes and mushrooms can sit in a cooler area. It may well be necessary to secure the food using wire ties as explained in the instructions section.

Ingredients

- *4 pork sausages*
- *6 small button mushrooms*
- *1 tomato, halved*
- *4 bacon rashers*
- *150g of black pudding*
- *butter*
- *salt and pepper*
- *a dash of sugar*
- *bread roll, to serve*

The 'Nearly Full' English Breakfast

Each of the core components of this meal will be cooked inside its own double wrapped tinfoil package. Double wrap all four pork sausages in tinfoil, and do the same for the black pudding. For the bacon rashers ensure that they only form a single layer when wrapping them in tinfoil so that they all cook evenly. On my tomatoes I always like to put a little salt and sugar on the top, with a dab of butter, then wrap well in tinfoil. Take the stalks of the mushrooms off, place a little butter in the bowl of the mushroom, and then wrap in tinfoil. As I mentioned before, when placing on the engine it is important to prioritise the sausages, bacon and black pudding onto the hottest parts of the engine. Then fit the tomatoes and mushrooms around where you can. Drive for one hour before serving on a buttered bread roll.

"One of the very nicest things about life is the way we must regularly stop whatever it is we are doing and devote our attention to eating."

– Luciano Pavarotti

Five-Spice Duck
Breasts with
Noodles.

1 Hour Drive
Serves: 2

Removing the duck fat is essential to this recipe as it won't crisp up in the tinfoil and no one wants soggy fat in a mouthful. This means that later in the week at home you can use that fat to crisp up your roast potatoes or parsnips. And in the meantime you can treat yourself to a sticky duck breast from the comfort of your own car. Accompanied with noodles and stir-fry vegetables, this Chinese meal is delicious. The rich taste of the duck breasts speak for themselves and little is needed to make this one a favorite dish of mine.

Ingredients

2 small duck breasts
4 tsp five-spice powder
2 tbsp clear honey
1 tsp soy sauce
400g fresh egg noodles
swig of toasted sesame seed oil (olive oil)
handful of sliced cabbage
½ pepper, finely chopped
handful of bean sprouts

Remove the fat from the duck breasts, and then smear the breasts with honey and Chinese five-spice. Add a little soy sauce and double wrap the breasts individually into tinfoil packaging. Add noodles to a tinfoil package and add a little toasted sesame seed oil, wrap well. Add vegetables to tinfoil and wrap carefully. Place all packages on the engine prioritising the duck breasts to the hottest part.

1 Hour and 20 minute Drive

Serves: 2

These lamb chops are a very elegant dish, which can easily impress with just a little effort. I like to leave my chops marinating overnight but it isn't essential. Setting off on a small journey, I had four hungry men sitting in the car. After announcing that in 40 minutes we would be eating the lamb chops that were currently sitting on the engine I received a torrent of abuse. "It won't work you idiot", "Can we please just go to McDonalds or something", "It'll taste like car fumes". After another half an hour's drive we found a spot for a little lunch and I opened the tinned foil to surprise and delight. I was very smug.

Ingredients

- *2 tbsp of chopped fresh mint*
- *2 tbsp chopped fresh rosemary*
- *a glug of olive oil*
- *4 cloves garlic, minced*
- *8 lamb chops (off the rib, or loin)*
- *2 courgette*
- *1 lemon*
- *salt and pepper*
- *pine nuts*
- *mint and beetroot puree (p78), to serve*
- *salsa verde (p80), to serve*

Lamb Cutlets with Courgette and Pine Nuts.

Finely chop the mint, rosemary and garlic, and add to a mixing bowl with the olive oil, a pinch of salt and a twist of pepper, and mix well. Score the chops and then rub the marinade into the meat. Ideally leave overnight, but for at least one hour. Fold the chops in a double layer of tinfoil ensuring that only 2 chops are packaged together, side-by-side. Finely slice the courgette and add a squeeze of lemon. Season well and then add the crushed pine nuts. Fold up and place all the packages on the car. Drive for an hour and twenty minutes before checking

V.W. PARKING ONLY
- Long Journeys -

1 Hour and 30 Minute Drive
Serves: 4

A Moroccan-enthused dish that combines sweet pomegranate seeds with spicy harissa. All snugly combined in a pitta wrap, this is a perfect thing for the road with no mess or hassle. The chunks of lamb can be cut smaller for a slightly quicker cooking time or alternatively can be cut into larger chunks for a longer journey. The pitta can be wrapped in tinfoil and put on a cooler part of the engine to warm them through although this is not essential. Yogurt is key for me, mainly because I can't handle the spice of the harissa so need some at the ready to pour down my throat before sweating and breathing heavily. I've somehow managed to make this one sound pretty disgusting but it's actually a fantastic meal.

Ingredients

400g boneless lamb leg, sliced/ shredded
2 chillies
2tsp thyme
2 tsp cumin
4 pitta flatbreads
1 carrot finely peeled
seeds of ½ a pomegranate
250g of greek yogurt
harissa (p88), to serve
olive oil
mint leaves
a squeeze of orange

Take the finely sliced lamb and cover with chilli, thyme and cumin. Double wrap in tin foil, making sure that the lamb is not overcrowded. Place on the engine and drive for an hour and thirty minutes. Finely peel the carrot, add a squeeze of an orange, mint leaves, and olive oil. Slit the pitta and open up to put the lamb inside. Sprinkle pomegranate seeds all over, and serve with yogurt and harissa to taste. Admire your food, before uploading a photo to Instagram to show off to all your friends.

1 Hour, 30 Minute Drive.
Serves: 2

Tomato, Pesto and Mozzarella Stuffed Aubergine.

I always think that stuffed aubergine looks a little scruffy and tastes very nice, but in this case I think that it looks very elegant. It is very important that the slits in the aubergines are cut as thinly as possible, otherwise it will not cook all the way through. The tomato and mozzarella must also be sliced very finely otherwise it begins to look like an oversized water balloon and may not fit as well in the engine. The classic combo of basil, mozzarella, and tomato, topped off with a little pesto makes for very delicious light lunch.

Ingredients
2 aubergines
2 tomatoes, sliced
1 ball of mozzarella, sliced
2 sprigs basil, torn
1 tbsp pesto (p78)
2 cloves of garlic, crushed

Cut the aubergines into 1.5cm wide slices keeping it adjoined at the stalk-end. Spoon a little pesto in between each layer of aubergine, and also add some crushed garlic. Then place the tomatoes and mozzarella slices between the layers of the aubergine. Season with salt and pepper. Double wrap both aubergines separately in tinfoil and add to the engine. Drive for one and half hours before eating.

Alternatively for a shorter cooking time you can cut the aubergines directly down the middle, and then spoon out some of middle of the aubergine. Into this place the tomatoes, garlic, basil, mozzarella, and pesto. These halves of aubergine then need to be double wrapped individually in tinfoil, and added to the engine before embarking on a one hour journey.

1 Hour and 40 Minute Drive
Serves: 3

This Hugh Fearnley-Whittingstall inspired lamb loin's flavours are similar to those found in a Northern African tagine, and certainly provide an unusually sweet but sharp taste. When producing a stuffing it is important to keep the quantity low and the flavours high so that you avoid bland mouthfuls of just stuffing and this recipe provides that rich flavour required.

I usually imagine eating the food in a romantic setting, with a typical English picnic scene in the background but sometimes time creeps up on you and you just have to pull over and eat. As I watched the traffic race by, I thought of all the wasted heat that was pouring out of the engines, and not being put to good use. It made me think how lucky I have been to stumble on this phenomenon.

Ingredients

500g of boned loin of lamb
20g pine nuts
1 tsp coriander seeds
1 tsp cumin seeds
a large knob of butter
2 spring onions, finely chopped
6 dried apricots, chopped
10g breadcrumbs
salt and pepper

North African Lamb Loin With Apricot and Pine Nuts.

Crush the pine nuts, coriander seeds and cumin seeds with a pestle and mortar (or with the back of a spoon on a wooden board). Add these to the butter, spring onions, finely-chopped apricots, and breadcrumbs.

Place the boned loin skin side down, and make a small incision along the length of the eye of the meat. Press a little of the stuffing into this slit and spread the rest evenly over the inside of the meat. Roll up the joint, with the eye in the centre, and tie it tight using butcher's string. Wrap the joint in tinfoil, ensuring a double layer of tinfoil on the top layer, but a single layer on the bottom. Place on the engine and drive for 1 hour and 40 minutes.

"The only real stumbling block is fear of failure. In cooking you've got to have a what-the-hell attitude."

-Julia Child

1 Hour and 50 Minute Drive
Serves: 4

A Chinese Take Away Pork Tenderloin with Noodles.

Pork tenderloin's flavour has never really inspired me, so it is important that you pack it full of interesting ingredients to liven it up. I focus on providing the sweet and sour combination with honey and ginger, and then add soy sauce and brown sugar for that sticky finish. I love having this with noodles, which are easily achieved on the engine if you use fresh noodles. I really enjoy a good Chinese and since they are often delivered by car, maybe soon the Chinese takeaway restaurants will just cook it on a car?

Ingredients
250g pork tenderloin, diced
1 tsp honey
2 tsp brown sugar
crushed peppercorns
a handful of wild mushrooms (shiitake, chestnut, oyster or girolle)
½ a red pepper, finely sliced
2 cloves garlic, crushed
400g fresh noodles
fish sauce
coriander
spring onions
soy sauce

Take the diced pork tenderloin and add the honey, brown sugar and the crushed peppercorns. Mix these ingredients together and then double wrap in tinfoil. Add the mushrooms, crushed garlic and sliced red pepper to a layer of tinfoil and wrap this in two layers of tinfoil. The moisture released from the mushrooms will make these very succulent. Finally add the fresh egg noodles to a layer of tinfoil and add a splash of fish sauce. Double wrap this in tin foil and you should now have 3 tinfoil packages that can be added to the engine. Drive for an hour and 50 minutes. On arriving take the packages off the engine. Add them all to a bowl and then garnish with coriander, spring onions and soy sauce to taste.

2 Hour Drive
Serves: 2

Similar to barbecuing, the fear of undercooking chicken hangs overhead, and often results in overcooked, dry, cardboardy meat. So the best way to overcome this issue is to cook the chicken in a moist sauce that would give the chicken flavour but also keep it succulent and fresh. Fajitas tackle these issues perfectly but do take a surprisingly long time. About 2 hours start to finish, but definitely worth the wait. There's something very satisfying about making these from scratch and even more satisfying if you have made the guacamole and tomato salsa too.

Chicken Fajitas with Guacamole, Salsa and Yogurt.

Ingredients

1 large chicken breast, diced
1 red pepper, diced
1 red onion, finely chopped
1 tsp paprika
a dash of ground cumin
a squeeze of lime
4 tortilla wraps
Cheddar, grated
soured cream
guacamole (p80), to serve
tomato salsa (p88), to serve

Add evenly-diced chicken breasts into a mixing bowl and add the chopped onions, peppers with the paprika and cumin. Toss thoroughly, ensuring an even covering of spice. Squeeze a little lime juice over the top, place in tinfoil and double wrap. Meanwhile, make up the guacamole and tomato salsa as explained in the sauces section. Place these in sealable boxes and then add them to the picnic basket with the tortilla wraps, cheddar, and soured cream. Place the tinfoil package containing the fajita mix onto the engine and drive for 2 hours. Unwrap the fajitas and then place the chicken into tortilla wraps and add sauces as you wish.

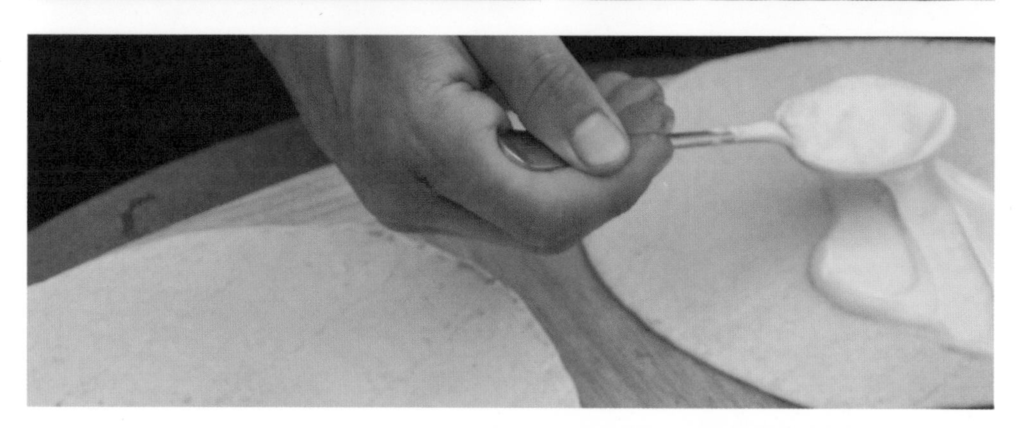

2 Hour Drive
Serves: 5

Honey and Mustard Glazed Gammon with Baked Potatoes.

With a quick stop off at the butcher before my journey to a fair in the heart of Scotland, I picked up a gammon joint and slathered it in honey and mustard before wrapping it up and sticking it on the engine, with baked potatoes also under the hood. ("Under the hood", I am so down with kids) An hour and a half later and I had a meal cooked for all of my passengers, but this can be cooked for up to 8. I was quite proud of this one. Succulent, cooked through with a piping hot potato served with butter. What made me even happier was that when we arrived the food van was selling a burger and chips for £5 per person. My meal had cost £5 for 6 people. This meal is cheap as chips (probably cheaper than the burger van's chips) and is exceedingly tasty.

Ingredients

1.2kg gammon joint
1 tbsp of honey
1 tbsp of mustard
5 baking potatoes
summer leaves, to serve
butter, to serve
salt and pepper
sweet chilli jam (p86), to serve
salsa verde (p80), to serve

Smear the honey and mustard all over the gammon joint and then double wrap in tinfoil. Individually double wrap each potato and then place all packages on the engine and drive for 1 and a half hours. Cut the ham into slices on arrival and add butter to the baked potato. I like to serve mine with some summer leaves or winter cabbage.

1 Hour, 45 Minutes- 3 Hour Drive
Serves: 4

While cooking ribs in tinfoil might not seem like the most desirable way to make them, I disagree. Cooking them surrounded by flavours that cannot escape the tinfoil's grasps only makes them tastier. Ok, so I'd give them a quick sizzle at the end to give them a charred edge but apart from that I'd really recommend doing them in tinfoil and therefore they suit Carbecue. There's not much better than sinking your teeth into a sweet rib and gently pulling the meat off the bone. I've never really met anyone who is disappointed when told they'll be having ribs for supper and these are no different. I'd also recommend doing these with a potato, pepper and onion mix.

Ingredients

British pork ribs (600g)
140g sweet chilli sauce
100g ketchup
zest and juice 3 limes
5tbsp soy sauce
1 tbsp of honey
1 tbsp of mustard
sprinkling of chilli flakes.

4 potatoes, sliced
2 cloves garlic, minced
1 medium onion
1 red bell pepper, chopped roughly
1 tablespoon fresh thyme
4 tablespoons butter
salt and pepper

Sweet Chilli Sticky Spare Ribs.

Mix the sweet chilli sauce, tomato ketchup, soy sauce, honey, mustard, and add the chilli flakes and the zest and juice of the limes. Rub the sauce into the ribs and leave in the fridge to marinate overnight or just for an hour or so if you're short of time. Meanwhile, take the potatoes, garlic, onion, pepper, thyme, butter, and season with salt and pepper. Then place on tinfoil and double wrap. Do the same with the marinated ribs, being sure not to overcrowd the tinfoil packages. I usually separate the ribs into two packages. Place on the engine for an hour and forty five minutes minimum. I have done them for up to 3 hrs, and it only makes the meat more tender, so this is perfect if you're not quite sure when you'll be hungry or find a nice place to stop.

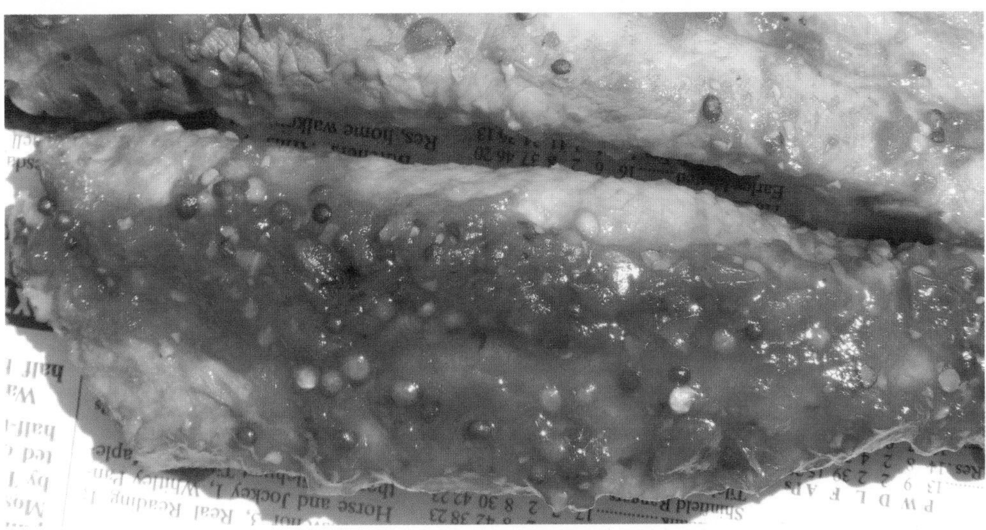

2 Hours, 30 Minutes to 3 Hours 30 Minute Drive
Serves: 4

There's something very British about cooking a roast on a car engine. I was meeting up with a few friends at the pub and thought that I'd cook a joint of roast beef as a little treat. As I opened up my bonnet to take the roast beef out, a member of the public came over to help assuming I must have engine trouble. I'll always remember the look of surprise on his face as I unwrapped a perfectly cooked rump of beef. The kind landlord let us eat it in the garden and we all had a merry time while treating ourselves to delicious rare roast beef. Ideal for a midway break on a long journey, this little gem is as easy as they come. I have always thought that beef is best cooked with no extravagance, because the meat provides enough flavors not to be messed about with. So forgive me if you think this is a little boring, but if you do want to liven it up, bring some horseradish with you to serve.

Ingredients

800g beef top rump joint
15- 20 baby new potatoes, halved
a couple of anchovies
a garnishing of rosemary
a drizzle of olive oil

choice of sauces to serve

horseradish (p82), to serve
salsa verde, (p80), to serve

Double wrap the beef fillet in tinfoil. Add the halved baby new potatoes to a seperate tinfoil package and sprinkle some chopped rosemary over the top. Add a few anchovies to provide a salty taste and then double wrap the package in tinfoil. Add both packages to the engine, ensuring that the beef is on the hottest part. Drive for at least two and half hours for a rare joint or up to three and a half for a more well done joint. I think that salsa verde is more or less essential for this meal, as it really provides something extra.

- Sauces -

These sauces are to be cooked at home and can be taken with you to liven up a Carbecue expedition.

Homemade Pesto

Ingredients
50g fresh basil
1 garlic clove, crushed
1 tbsp pine nuts
6 tbsp olive oil
50g Parmesan, grated
salt

I like homemade pesto and the fun you can have making different variations, depending on what you need to get rid of. I sometimes make it with coriander and almonds, instead of basil and pine nuts, for an interesting change. Walnuts and hazelnuts work too. Store in the fridge and it should keep for at least three days.

Put the basil, garlic, pine nuts and olive oil into a food blender. Blend until in a smooth puree and then add the Parmesan and salt to taste. Stir until well mixed and serve.

Served with:
Stuffed Aubergine (p60)
Couscous (p38)

Mint and Beetroot Purée

Ingredients
600g cooked beetroot
a large bunch of mint
a small handful of coriander
1 tbsp olive oil
a squeeze of lemon juice
salt and pepper

I cheat and use vacuum packed pre-cooked beetroot although you could cook it yourself if you've got a little more time on your hands by wrapping it in tinfoil and baking it. This vibrant dip is very refreshing and with Instagram demanding beautiful presentation of food this can help liven up an otherwise dull plate. The joys of modern life.

Add all the ingredients to a food processer and blend until smooth. Taste and add salt accordingly. I find that quite a lot of salt is needed.

Served with:
Lamb Cutlets (p54)

Guacamole

I always think that less is more with guacamole and that the rich and creamy flavour of the avocado should not be complicated with too many ingredients. I like to mash the avocado very lightly so that I leave the occasional chunk of avocado. This only takes a couple of minutes to prepare and is an absolute essential for Fajitas.

Ingredients

1 large avocado
1 tbsp olive oil
a bunch of coriander/parsley
a squeeze of lime juice
salt and pepper

Remove the flesh from the avocado and mash it with a fork. Add the chopped parsley or coriander, olive oil and squeeze the lime juice over the lot, and mix well. Season. *Viola!*

Served with:
Fajitas (p68)

Salsa Verde

Ingredients

2 cloves of garlic
a few capers
a tin of anchovy fillets
a bunch of flat parsley, basil, mint.
a tbsp Dijon mustard
3 tbsp red wine vinegar
8 tbsp good olive oil

This is without a doubt my favorite sauce. It can liven up anything that is a touch bland, or complement anything tasty. I use mine with beef, lamb, potatoes, chicken, couscous – anything really. Feel free to vary the amount of each herb, I often make it with lots of mint and sometimes add coriander too. It should keep for about a week in a fridge, but usually doesn't last that long without being eaten.

Served with:
Roast Beef (p74)
Lamb Cutlets (p54)
Honey and Mustard Gammon (p70)

In a food processer blend all the above ingredients. I usually add the oil as I go, so that I don't overdo it. Simples.

Cucumber and Dill Sauce

I think that dill is a very underused herb and should be one of the staples for cooks across the country. This sauce is perfect for salmon but can also liven up potatoes, give fajitas a bit of a twist, or even put on lamb chops. It's what I would describe as a cooling sauce and is therefore very good accompanied with a spicy meal.

Ingredients
½ cucumber
1 pinch salt
Black pepper, freshly ground
250g plain yoghurt
2 tsp Dijon mustard
1 spring onion, finely chopped
1 tbsp dill, chopped

Served with:
Salmon (p24)

Dice the cucumber, and place in a sieve. Salt the cucumber and leave for up to an hour. Rinse to remove the salt and then dry with kitchen paper. Stir the cucumber well with the yogurt, mustard, spring onion and dill, and season to taste.

Horseradish Cream

I've always hated the sensation of peeling onions and having tears streaming down my cheeks, but it is nothing compared to the sensation that grating horseradish creates. Rather than tears it feels more like your eyeballs are melting, and slowly dribbling out of their sockets. I therefore cheat and put all the ingredients into a blender and then disappear into the garden while I wait for the fumes to clear.

Ingredients
100g freshly grated horseradish root
a pinch of sugar
2 tsp cider vinegar
1 tsp hot English mustard
125g crème fresh
sea salt and freshly ground black pepper

Blend the horseradish, sugar, vinegar, and mustard together and leave to macerate for half an hour before folding in the crème fresh. Season to taste. Refrigerate and use within 24 hours.

Served with:
Roast Beef (p74)

"Food for thought is no substitute for the real thing."
-Walt Kelly

Redcurrant Jelly

I love recipes with only two real ingredients. It makes you realise just how easy cooking is, and left me wondering why you'd ever buy supermarket redcurrant jelly again.

Wash the redcurrants and discard any rotten ones. Add them to a large pot – stalks and all – and then add 1 cm of water to the bottom of the pan. Slowly bring to the boil, and then simmer for approximately ten minutes until all the fruit is cooked. Add the sugar and then stir until all the sugar is entirely dissolved. Then bring to a rapid boil and continue boiling for eight minutes. After this place a large sieve over a bowl. Now pour the whole contents of the pan into the bowl through the sieve. Avoid the temptation to push the redcurrants, as you will end up with murky jelly. Now pour the jelly into clean jars, which have been heated in an oven for five minutes to sterilise them, and seal the lids firmly.

Ingredients
800g redcurrants
800g of sugar
water

Served with:
Lamb cutlets (p75)

Sweet Chilli Jam

This provides a nice sweet, spicy combination and for those of you wanting to liven up a few of the recipes, this is the perfect treat. Should keep in the larder for months and is a very good way of preserving tomatoes.

Blend 400g whole tomatoes, four chillies (seeds and all), six cloves of garlic, two small knobs of ginger (don't bother to peel them), & 30 ml of Thai fish sauce (half a little bottle). Put this in a saucepan with 450g ordinary sugar, and 8 tbsp red wine vinegar. Bring to a simmer. Meanwhile, finely chop another 400g tomatoes. Add them to the pan, and gently simmer for at least an hour, stirring occasionally. You have to judge for yourself when it's cooked, and it may well take longer than an hour to reach a set (it will set without trouble, because tomatoes are full of pectin).

Ingredients
800g whole tomatoes
four chillies
6 cloves garlic
2 small knobs ginger
30 ml Thai fish sauce
450g sugar
8tbsp red wine vinegar

Served with:
Stuffed Mushrooms (p34)
Oriental Seabass (p36)
Beef Burger (p42)
Tuna Burger (p44)
Honey and Mustard Gammon (p70)

Tomato Salsa

Salsa is incredibly refreshing, particularly when made from scratch. This can be used as a dip, in fajitas, with a burger, in a sandwich, or even as a side salad for any meal really. Very versatile and very easy. You can mix it up and try using parsley instead of coriander or maybe add some mozzarella if you want it as a side salad.

Ingredients

4 ripe tomatoes, chopped
half a red onion, chopped
1 clove garlic
1 chilli (or less, if you're feeling particularly pathetic)
a bunch of coriander

Served with:
Fajitas (p68)
Beef Burger (p74)
Tuna Burger (p44)

Finely chop the tomatoes, red onion, chilli and coriander. Then crush the garlic and mix all the ingredients together well.

Harrissa Paste

Ingredients

75g red chillies
4 large garlic cloves, peeled
75g onion roughly chopped
1 tsp cumin seeds, ground
1 tsp coriander seeds, ground
salt
400g tin of good quality chopped tomatoes
75g red wine vinegar

This is a Northern African inspiration and has become increasingly popular in recent years. It complements lamb, beef and couscous particularly well, but can also be rubbed onto meat before cooking it, to liven it up.

Put all the ingredients into a food blender and blitz until quite smooth. Taste and adjust if necessary. When suitable to taste add to a pan and boil until thick. You will need to stir frequently, until the liquid at the top disappears. Decant into jars and put a little olive oil on top. Makie sure it's covered with oil after every time you use it and it will keep for months in the fridge.

Served with:
Lamb Kebab (p58)

"One cannot think well, love well, sleep well, if one has not dined well."
-Virginia Woolf
Wild Garlic Yarg
(Pengreep, Cornwall)
Past. Cow's
£2.20/100g
Parmiagiano Reggiano
(Parmesan)
(Parma Italy)